AARC

Ena Manning.
100 Springfort
Meadows
Nenagh

067 34157.

First published 2008 by
Veritas Publications
7/8 Lower Abbey Street
Dublin 1
Ireland
Email publications@veritas.ie
Website www.veritas.ie

ISBN 978 1 84730 122 2

Copyright © Marguerite Kiely, 2008

10 9 8 7 6 5 4 3 2 1

Designed by Barbara Croatto
Printed in the Republic of Ireland by ColourBooks Ltd, Dublin

Veritas books are printed on paper made from the wood pulp of managed
forests. For every tree felled, at least one tree is planted, thereby renewing
natural resources.

AARON'S LEGACY

His presence an inspiration, and everlasting,
through the birth of a dream

MARGUERITE KIELY

VERITAS

This book is dedicated to the staff and medical team
of Bristol hospital and of CLIC House.
To those parents who shared our journey with their own pain. To my sisters and brothers: a
thank you from Aaron for the love, tears, but most of all the fun you each shared with him.
To Austin, Colin, Chloe and Ava: in each of you Aaron continues to smile each day. To my
parents Peter and Madge: cradle my boy in your arms. Finally, to all those who work with
such compassion and dedication providing the wonderful facility of Brú Columbanus.

CONTENTS

CHAPTER I

LOVING YOU IS SHARING YOU

It's 27 September 2005 and we're travelling back from Cork to our home in Dublin. It's a damp, misty night. I turn and look behind to see my two daughters, both exhausted after this busy but special day. Chloe, ten years, covered with her favourite pink fluffy blanket, her straight blonde hair swept across the pillow that accompanied her on all her travels. Ava, just two years old, propped up in her car seat with her pink 'duddy' moving up and down in her mouth, her sweaty tangled blonde curls framing her peaceful face. I smiled, for today I could see my darling Aaron within them both. Chloe with her everlasting patience and gentleness, Ava with those vivid blue eyes reminiscent of his wonderful, handsome expression, an expression I was once told was 'just too good looking for this world'.

Turning back, I stared at the raindrops racing down the car door window, and outside there was nothing but darkness, reflecting my own feeling of sadness. Words that angered me eleven years previously and that I had buried had today returned to life. Their meaning, so clearly evident and justified now, no longer accompanied by past pain but rather by a tremendous warmth and comfort which filled my every sense. 'Some day, I promise you, some good will come from this pain. Maybe not today, nor tomorrow, but it will come.'

It was Friday morning, 1 October 1993, 8 a.m., and my son, my darling Aaron, just eleven months old, was cradled in my arms, now at peace. Tears rolled down my face as Dr Ramaille uttered these words, gently rubbing my hand. His big soft brown eyes stared into mine, filled with emotion and sharing my unbearable grief. A pain he had seen so many times, but from which he was never detached. He was a Spanish intern who each morning and last thing at night came to our room on the oncology ward at Bristol Hospital for Sick Children, St Michael's Hill. He had developed a soft spot for Aaron and his 'crazy Irish family'. Today his words had come to fruition, the passage not fading their impact. This Monday morning had seen the opening of Brú Columbanus, a home-away-from-home for the families of the terminally ill. In memory of Aaron, this fabulous and much-needed facility had become the dream of my brother, Charlie, and now the object through which Dr Ramaille's prediction was turned into a reality. I had unveiled a plaque with the inscription: 'His presence an inspiration and everlasting'.

Oh his presence! For today, deep within me, I knew he had returned to this world, his love just too precious to lay to rest. I felt him near me so much this day I could once again smell his golden hair and feel the gentle softness of his skin against mine. Part of me wanted to cry out that he was back, but no, I was too greedy to share him. I needed so much to hold on to the amazing feeling of his warm presence.

Austin was driving and there was little chat between us. I knew how difficult the day had been for him. I sighed and he took my hand and asked if I was okay. I nodded; words were not needed for we both knew we were today back at a place of indescribable loss, a sadness the years hadn't erased, but had instead been replaced by a kind of acceptance that allows you to continue. Time does not pause for grief. My own belief is that it is nature's way of preventing you from going mad from the pain of a broken heart. I sighed again, my mind running back over that horrible time.

We had moved to Taunton in Somerset in 1990 when Austin was offered a job with Kerry Foods Plc. Colin, our first-born, was four years old and ready to begin school, so the timing for a change in our lives seemed perfect. For the first three months Austin had travelled back and forth from our home in Cork until he had found somewhere for us to live. We decided it was best to rent for a while, to allow us time to settle in and become accustomed to our new life. Taunton, the main town of Somerset, was a typical English town set in a picturesque landscape. It was small and easy to find your way round, which reminded me of my own home, Cork city. We enrolled Colin in Manor School, a small family-run country school, and he adapted easily. At this time we lived in the suburb of Galmington, an attractive new housing development, and in those first few months a neighbour, Jane Aldawani, came and introduced herself. Her little boy Adam travelled with Colin on the school bus, and Jane herself was a kind, gentle lady who was to become a great friend and support in the difficult times ahead.

After the initial period of excitement and busyness with our new home I began to experience bouts of incredible loneliness. I missed my family back in Ireland, and telephone bills were a constant source of discussion, but Austin always took pity and succumbed to the charges! There were also other Irish families working within the company and living close by. In time we developed a good social life with those whom I refer to as 'some of my own'. It was the first time that I had, however, also experienced a divide in cultures, a shock to me as our countries were so close in proximity. At times I felt alienated because of my strong Irish accent. This was the period during which to be Irish in England automatically linked you with the Troubles. When I had to explain the geographical location of Cork to my neighbours I became aware of how limited they were in their knowledge of Ireland.

In 1992 we decided we would like a brother or sister for Colin. I remember how excited he was when I told him I was pregnant; he couldn't wait to tell all his friends on the school bus and he wrote it on his news board in class that day.

My pregnancy went extremely well and my gynaecologist and GP never had any cause for concern at any stage. I enjoyed being pregnant and deep down I longed for a baby girl and spent a lot of time looking at pink clothes. Little did I know that this small, insignificant desire would in future years haunt me with an overwhelming sense of guilt.

It was during my pregnancy that I met Dr John Scanlon, a Limerick GP living in Taunton. Because of his Irish origins we developed a friendly rapport and he would soon become a strong anchor in our lives. And on reflection, life was kind to us at that time: we had our health and our family situation was so very normal, so very good.

CHAPTER II

AARON'S DIAGNOSIS
Parents' Disbelief

November 5, I arrived at Musgrove General Hospital, Taunton, Somerset, two weeks overdue and grateful to be induced. I had had an easy birth with Colin, who was born in Cork, and so I was not prepared for the idea that labour can be very difficult and very painful. I remember the anaesthetist arriving to give me my epidural, which had worked wonders with Colin. Initially everything went according to plan, but ten minutes later my blood pressure dropped considerably. I began shaking uncontrollably and vomiting. I could see Austin growing paler and there was a sense of panic in the room as my baby became distressed. My gynaecologist was brought in and it took thirty minutes before I stabilised. The epidural failed to relieve the pain and I gave birth lying on my side as every time I turned on my back my blood pressure dropped dramatically. Aaron arrived at 1:40 a.m., and a welcome sight he was, crying and a lovely pink colour. All was well with him, but I didn't produce the placenta and was taken to theatre, legs in stirrups, an experience that remained with me for months after.

I often wondered if the trauma of his birth contributed to the development of Aaron's disease, a question the oncologist could never confirm nor deny as studies at the time had only just started including such data. But I remember just how beautiful he was, with slight wisps of golden hair, a beautifully shaped head and big open eyes. Jane, who worked at the hospital, arrived shortly after the birth and as she cradled Aaron she nicknamed him 'Sparky' because it was Guy Fawkes day. Colin was delighted with his new brother, and how grown up he felt as he held Aaron in his small arms, dangling his own

13
—

little legs over the side of my bed. He was as proud as Austin, whose beaming smile revealed his own joys.

Three weeks later, Aaron Noel was christened by my brother Fr Noel; both my sisters, Bernadette and Colette, and my mum and brother-in-law Maurice attended the celebration. Maurice became Aaron's godfather and Colette was proud to be godmother. It was a joyful occasion.

Aaron was a good baby, loved his bottles and slept well at night. As the months went by he developed into a handsome little guy, adored by Colin. I was a stay-at-home mum and my world centred around the boys. When Aaron was three months old I flew with both the boys back to Cork to introduce Aaron to his cousins and spend time with his grandparents. I remember him stretched out on his blue blanket on my sister's lounge floor, surrounded by cuddly toys, gifts that had awaited his arrival. He was such a jolly little chap, all smiles, and how he kicked those legs when excited. I had two lovely boys, exhausting at times, but my fondest memories would be of them both splashing around at bath time and Colin feeding Aaron his bedtime bottle, propped up with pillows on my bed. I often felt proud of Colin and how he never displayed jealousy towards his baby brother; though I can vividly recall those mornings when Colin would get annoyed by Aaron's 'chatting', put him in his bouncer out in the hallway and bang the lounge door. It was so funny to see little Aaron sitting there in complete silence, shocked by Colin's abandonment and awaiting his return, unaware that by now Colin was too engrossed in his favourite 'Teenage Mutant Ninja Turtles' cartoon!

My times alone with Aaron were spent walking along a nearby canal where we would go to visit the ducks. His eyes would light up in excitement as they approached his buggy. Other days we would travel into town and visit a great children's boutique, called 'Little Ones'. Aaron was by this time a recognised customer, and Helena, the owner, referred to him as Robert Redford's child, because of his blond hair and blue eyes. In the courtyard there was a lovely coffee shop where we would meet our friends. Aaron would be on my lap devouring his yoghurt, and we would watch the world go by. Taunton was especially beautiful in the springtime, with flowers in bloom everywhere.

The weather was mild in the spring of 1993. Our weekends were spent travelling to various new places like Devon and Cornwall, Cheddar and the beautiful city of Exeter. Aaron loved travelling in the car and I often recall turning round to see Colin sharing his ice-cream and Aaron screaming with delight at being allowed a few licks. April and May were busy months with Colin having school plays and family days. As I sat in the school assembly hall with Aaron snuggled in my arms there were many visits from Colin's friends to peer at his new baby brother; mothers would also gather to quiz me on his sleeping pattern and comment on how content he looked and how he loved his cuddles.

Blue was without doubt Aaron's colour; by five months all his baby suits had been replaced with what Colin referred to as 'his boy clothes'. He was very dapper in his ensembles of shorts and t-shirts, a peak cap often adorning his blond head. Colin used to get a great kick out of one specific check shirt, red and blue in colour. He compared it to one worn by my own father, and so would associate Aaron's chubby cheeks with his grandfather's ageing jowls!

During these first six months Aaron never had a sick day, never a cough or a cold, and took his vaccines well. I never at any stage had the slightest worry, and illness was not a word I associated with my baby. However, that was to change, and our safe, ever so normal life was about to be encased in the most unbearable pain imaginable.

June was a particularly warm month. We had by this stage moved to our new home, which had a large garden. I looked forward to spending the summer days sitting on the patio watching the boys enjoying the new play area we had built for them. It was, however, at this time that I noticed that Aaron was napping a little longer than usual. His one-hour nap at lunchtime now lasted two to two-and-a-half hours. Though I was initially grateful for this, there were times when I would have to go and wake him. I noticed that he was not crying out 'Momma' when he woke but instead simply lay in his cot listless. While out walking he wasn't as stimulated as before and during our travels in the car his usual chatter was replaced with naps. But he was drinking his bottles and eating well, and when I mentioned to friends that he seemed a little withdrawn, they would try to put me at ease, saying I just had an exceptionally placid baby. Deep down I knew something was wrong; the sparkle in his eyes seemed dimmer each day and I wasn't happy with his pale colour.

I decided to have him checked by my GP, so I went along to a morning surgery. Aaron seemed content and at one stage I considered going home. As I sat in the waiting room the sounds of chesty coughs and fevered whines from the other children and babies there seemed much more urgent. I felt silly that I might be wasting my time but decided I had spent enough nights wondering about the change in Aaron.

This was our first consultation, and it was with an unfamiliar doctor as my own GP wasn't there that day. I voiced my concerns, explaining the changes in Aaron over the previous fortnight. I held Aaron in my arms as his ears, throat and temperature were examined. I was uneasy and noticed that the doctor didn't establish eye contact with me nor listen carefully to what I was describing. I also noticed and found it unusual that he never took Aaron from my arms to examine him. He diagnosed that Aaron might have the tail end of a virus, but as long as he was drinking and feeding he was not unduly concerned. I felt like the paranoid mother, but relieved.

Our first consultation had lasted a brief ten minutes, but in the following months its repercussions were to engulf me in a paralysing rage; I could not let it go. I would learn in future months from Aaron's oncologist that at this particular stage Aaron was anaemic and a good GP would have detected this following my concerns over his sleeping pattern, and by conducting a simple test of pressing his thumb against my baby's foot and noticing no healthy pink colour.

I returned home from the doctor's surgery and Austin agreed Aaron was not himself and suggested that we make a second appointment with my usual doctor on his return. This, unfortunately, was not to be.

It was Thursday night, 6 July. I bathed both Aaron and Colin, and noticed that Aaron seemed a little restless. That evening I had arranged for my friend Jane to visit and I was looking forward to a good chat. When Jane arrived Aaron was crying, which was so unlike him, so I took him from his cot and Jane played with him as I prepared his bottle. When I tried to feed him he seemed more distressed and we sensed that he was in pain. He kicked his legs straight out and his body seemed to freeze. I brought him upstairs to my bed to remove his baby suit as I wondered if it was restricting his movement. I will never forget the appearance of his stomach when I removed his clothes: it was protruding like that of a malnourished African child and I could clearly see the veins along it. I remember running to Jane and putting him in her arms as I rang Dr Scanlon. He could sense the panic in my voice and assured me that he would be with me within ten minutes. Those ten minutes were a lifetime. Jane and I stood there trying to convince each other that it was some sort of colicky spasm. At this stage Austin was also on his way home, fearing that things were a lot more serious. Dr Scanlon examined Aaron very briefly, then admitted him to hospital, and though he never gave an opinion as to what it might be wrong, I could hear the urgency in his voice. Austin and I agreed it would be faster for us to take him ourselves than wait for an ambulance. I went on autopilot, packing the baby's bag and trying to find his favourite toys, as Jane followed me around and attempted to ease my panic. She agreed to stay with Colin while Austin and I were at the hospital.

Musgrove Hospital. Thankfully I had never had much need to visit and this was my first time back since Aaron's birth. It was 10 p.m. and the A&E was exceptionally quiet. The air of panic around me seemed to diminish as Aaron had at this point settled a bit and was sleeping in Austin's arms. At reception we signed the usual forms and were met by a nurse who had earlier spoken to Dr Scanlon. She showed us into a small private room and told us that Aaron was booked for an x-ray and scan, and that they were waiting for the radiographer. It didn't concern me that the radiographer was contacted especially. Aaron was now awake and playing with Austin, but the atmosphere was tense and silent. I can still so clearly see Austin whispering every now and then in Aaron's ear, 'You're going to be alright, baby'. I went walking around the foyer and got talking to a young couple in their early twenties who were cuddling their two-year-old girl. I sat with them for a while and they explained that they were awaiting test results and feared their child might have meningitis. The nurse had gone to allocate them a room, and as their little girl started to cry in a high-pitched tone, the parents became agitated by the slowness of the staff. I tried to converse with them and comfort them, and spoke of how my little boy was now more settled following the panic of a couple of hours before. In hindsight I was comforting myself, trying to hide my fears.

We went with Aaron for his scan. It seemed to take ages and the radiographer was serious and intense, fully concentrating on her work. I asked the nurse on the way back to the room if we could take Aaron home and return in the morning. She advised us that it would be best to keep him overnight and that a doctor would visit us shortly. Aaron took his bottle and fell asleep in Austin's arms. Every now and then the nurse would pop her head in, smile gently at Aaron and ask if we needed anything. She explained it would be a while before all the test results would be back and sympathised with the waiting involved. I spent the next couple of hours walking empty corridors and absently reading the public notices. I would return to Austin every now and then, saying how ridiculous it was waiting when we lived so near and could be back first thing in the morning.

Aaron was sleeping well, so around 4.30 a.m. I decided to make a quick dash home to prepare Colin's school clothes and lunch. Alone in the kitchen, buttering bread, my mind was racing. I jumped when Jane arrived and as she stood against the counter top I scurried around the kitchen banging presses, giving out about being kept in the hospital probably just to be told to go home in the morning.

At 5.30 a.m. I returned to find Austin changing Aaron. We both studied his tummy, and although it felt hard it didn't appear as distended as it had been earlier. I went to the sink to wash my hands and it was then that the hidden fears came to life. My GP, looking tired and dressed in casual clothes, walked towards the nurse's desk, and as he approached he glanced towards me and our eyes locked. In those few moments everything around me seemed to slow down. I turned to Austin and told him that something was really wrong. While Dr Scanlon spoke to the staff nurse I tried desperately to interpret by their body language what they might have been discussing. I searched for a smile that might have signalled a friendly, relaxed chat, but as the doctor studied the paperwork the nodding of his head was ever so subdued. My heart began to pace and I nervously bit my lower lip. Dr Scanlon was then met by a more formally dressed man, stocky and in his late fifties. They shook hands and spoke intensely as they stood peering at the x-ray viewer. I could feel Austin's breath on the back of my neck and he questioned why Dr Scanlon was here so early. I turned and took Aaron and walked to the opposite corner of the room, protecting him as a lioness would her cub. The door opened and Dr Scanlon, the staff nurse and Mr Brennan, the hospital's chief consultant, entered. Mr Brennan suggested that the staff nurse hold Aaron and that both myself and Austin sit down. My eyes fixed on Dr Scanlon. My body felt drained of blood and my legs went to jelly. Mr Brennan explained how a large mass was covering Aaron's liver. He continued to speak but I heard nothing after the words 'tumour' and 'cancer'. I wanted to tell him to shut the hell up, but the lump in my throat wouldn't budge. I continued to focus on Dr Scanlon standing in the corner, but then the tears filled my eyes. He knew I wasn't listening any more and he looked at me and said gently, 'I'm really so very sorry'. I looked at the nurse as she gazed at Aaron's beautiful face and then I turned to Austin, who was still listening intently to Mr Brennan. He put his arms around me, pulled me towards him, and we were united in the knowledge that our beautiful baby boy was very ill. Dr Brennan then explained how Bristol Hospital for Sick Children was world-renowned for its excellent paediatric oncology treatments and research into children's cancers. He suggested we have Aaron transferred there immediately, and he then allowed us some time on our own to come to terms with this shock diagnosis.

I took Aaron from the nurse and sat with him in my arms, and I couldn't keep from kissing his forehead, my tears falling on him. Austin was kneeling beside me, rubbing Aaron's blond hair as his eyes also filled with tears. I felt I was dreaming and wanted desperately to feel the pain of someone slapping my face to wake me up. But we knew this was our new reality, that there were no choices or options and no turning back. At times I tried to compose myself by thinking of all the practical arrangements that would need to be made, but my mind was overwhelmed and my legs felt numb as I walked up and down the room.

I started getting agitated with myself because I couldn't think straight. I worried about Colin: what we would say to him, who would look after him; about Austin and the time he would need off from work. Austin reassured me that whatever was needed would be done and that getting Aaron well would be our first priority. I tried to speak rationally and clearly but I could not finish a sentence: I just cried and cried and cried. When the nurse brought tea and attempted to comfort me I just wanted her to go, to leave me alone. Suddenly I felt so vulnerable, so small, and I cried out to Austin that I needed my mother. Austin felt it would be best to contact my sister Bernadette and for her to break the news to my parents. He left me for a short while before returning to tell me that Bernadette would be catching a flight to Bristol that same day. It was such a relief knowing she would soon be alongside us.

CHAPTER III

BRISTOL HOSPITAL
In Search of Hope

Bristol was a city we had never visited though it was only an hour's drive up the M5. We had decided to take Aaron ourselves rather than have him go by ambulance, as he was now more comfortable. We left for the hospital at lunchtime and as we drove I held Aaron in my arms in the back seat. I kept rubbing his face and kissing his forehead, smelling that beautiful baby smell. My heart was breaking as I knew we weren't going to a place of fun, no theme park or zoo today. I knew I was taking him to an unfamiliar place with unfamiliar people, and that that night he would not be sleeping in his cosy cot nor would we have our normal evening routine. Driving through Bristol under the famous Clifton Bridge I stared out at ordinary people going about their normal lives. How I wanted to be part of this: putting Aaron in his buggy, scurrying around like all the other shoppers. I felt a sense of unrealism now, of being outside of this normal world, merely observing.

St Michael's Hill, a long, steep hill, is in the suburbs of Bristol, and Bristol Hospital for Sick Children stands on the left side as it evens out. To me it looked like an old orphanage from some black and white movie. Three large sets of stone steps led to high wooden doors, and I noticed parents and relatives huddled around wooden benches on each side of the entrance. It would be here over the next three months that I would many times sit with family and friends, simply to have a cry or to gain strength to return to the oncology ward. It would also be a place of laughter, a much-needed respite, and humour, which I soon found out was necessary to keep you sane. We were greeted by friendly staff and led to the oncology ward on the third floor; we had now entered into the world of childhood cancer.

It was a bright open ward with three large private rooms to the left, opening into a spacious area containing eight beds. These were surrounded by big windows that gave a fabulous, expansive view of Bristol City. It was such a busy ward; cartoons played on TVs as children and their parents all immersed in the hospital routine. As we stood holding Aaron at the nurse's desk I couldn't concentrate on her words to us. Looking around I began to experience my very first panic attack. My heart raced, I couldn't breathe, I felt physically sick. I was overwhelmed by all the ill children with bald heads and pale complexions. I went into complete denial, convincing myself that my baby didn't belong here.

We were led into a small room as the kind nurse explained we would soon meet Professor Mott, Head of the Oncology Department. While we were waithing I repeatedly told Austin and was adamant that we were taking Aaron to Great Ormond Street Hospital in London. Little did I know how in the following months I would become comfortably institutionalised within these walls, accustomed to every sound and action of the daily routine. I would become so familiar with all members of staff, both medical and domestic, with priests and social workers, but most importantly with parents just like us. All those who through their own special uniqueness transformed this ward into a wonderful world of care and compassion, which would make me feel so ashamed of my initial reaction.

It was now eight in the evening and I hadn't even unpacked the smallest of items, so intent was I on leaving. Aaron was sitting in his bouncer within his cot, playing with his favourite blue teddy. He wasn't at all distressed and was happily looking out at everyone as they passed his window. Bernadette arrived and we both burst into tears. She hadn't seen Aaron for a few months and was amazed at how big he'd grown and how handsome he was. He smiled brightly back at her as if in recognition and she cuddled and played with him. Soon afterwards Professor Mott arrived, accompanied by the staff nurse on duty. He sat with us, and I could sense his gentle, warm aura. He spoke softly and immediately put us at ease in his presence. He explained as simply as possible that Aaron's scan had shown a large mass on his liver, and that because of its size and position he was almost certain that it was malignant, but that a biopsy would be required to confirm this. My knowledge of cancer was very limited and it had never before been part of my world, but as he described the type of tumour, the idea of a liver transplant entered my head. I asked if Aaron would be a candidate for this, and he, realising my despair, spoke of other options open to us before going down that route. Hearing the word options, plural, immediately introduced hope, and hope was all we had to cling to now. It was explained that Aaron would need a course of chemotherapy, which would hopefully shrink the tumour. Professor Mott felt that Aaron's tumour might be classified as a 'hepaplastoma' and there would be a specific drug protocol to correspond with this type. He drew a diagram explaining that if the tumour originated to the left or right lobe of Aaron's liver, treatment might reduce the size, and surgery would be an option as the liver can regenerate itself. However, if the origin of the tumour was directly in the centre, things would be more complicated. He explained also that a Hickman line would be inserted in Aaron's chest to prepare for the administration of chemotherapy.

After Professor Mott's visit we felt a lot more at ease and confident that, though we had a difficult road ahead of us, things might work out. From that moment I focused on Professor Mott, willing him to give us our miracle. On reflection it was such a heavy and unfair burden to put on him, but desperation gives you permission to do these unreasonable things.

When I think about it now, that very first weekend in Bristol we were a family spun up in a whirlpool of emotion, and today it still amazes me how the human brain and body are capable of performing their duties on a daily basis. I still got up and showered, went to the shops for Aaron's favourite goodies (how excited he became when he got a glimpse of that Cadbury's chocolate and how it broke my heart in the months to follow when he refused it).

Those initial days Aaron settled quickly but the right side of his stomach was still swollen. Austin, Bernadette and I spent those first nights analysing every word Professor Mott uttered, convincing ourselves that all would be successful and agreeing to take a day at a time, as if we had any choice in that. We soon became familiar with the nursing staff because of their frequent visits to take bloods and carry out the other usual procedures. They would always leave the room commenting on Aaron's placid nature and beautiful eyes. Many a time it would be said that he would break a few hearts. I welcomed those kind words but knew the first heart had already been shattered and would never mend.

Bernadette was always by my side and had the wonderful ability of gathering information on the hospital procedures because of her natural interaction with both families and staff. We used visit a small local coffee shop for supplies and would do this in turns so that Aaron was never left on his own. It was at this time that I developed the art of becoming what I firmly believe was the world's fastest eater. I would rush back from any trip for sustenance just to be in Aaron's presence and play peek-a-boo with him. Austin would bring Colin in the evenings, along with some of Aaron's toys. At first Colin was taken aback by the ward, but following a trip to the shop for some sweeties he adjusted and took no notice. I knew how much of an upheaval it had all been to Colin's routine and how difficult it must have been for him with all attention now focused on Aaron, but we were determined not to let Colin be forgotten or become a background figure. Bernadette was also very aware of this, so he received bucketfuls of love and attention.

On Saturday afternoon Aaron was taken to The Royal Bristol Infirmary, the main hospital, located at the bottom of the hill. Here he would have his biopsy and his Hickman line fitted. We were allowed to go into the theatre with him and hold his hand as he drifted into sleep. I felt so helpless and guilty seeing him so small and defenceless surrounded by six or seven staff. I kissed him goodbye, and walking towards the doors I turned to look at him and the tears welled up. Two hours later he was back in my arms and, as I pressed him against my chest, I could feel what I now hoping would be his lifeline and cure. Family and friends showed great concern, but at times the telephone calls were exhausting. It was hard on my parents and immediate family back in Ireland waiting for the next bit of news.

By 8.00 a.m. the ward was already bustling. Domestic staff arrived, and though very welcoming of the new arrival I could also sense their sorrow at the fate of yet another new patient. Aaron was sitting in his bouncer, totally mesmerised by the fitness guru Mr Motivator on GMTV! We would laugh at Aaron's entranced expression and how, even as his bloods were being taken, he would strain his head around the nurse to continue watching the screen. Shortly afterwards Professor Mott arrived accompanied by his team of consultants and he introduced us to Dr Annadel Foot. She was a tall, slim, distinguished lady in her forties who would in the future months be the bearer of both good and bad news. We developed a strong relationship with her and had great admiration for how she sympathised with the pain of all the families and was never devoid of compassion. She was to meet with us again that afternoon when we would be informed of Aaron's biopsy results.

It was late in the afternoon when she returned to us and asked that we join her in her small office. I soon came to learn that a call to her office generally indicated bad news. This Monday evening was the beginning of many such visits. I recall now always leaving her room short of breath and hating God.

That first day Dr Foot explained how Aaron's tumour histology had revealed a large malignant mass on his liver, but that a difficulty had arisen in determining its classification. As a result of this it would be harder to match it with a known chemotherapy. We felt so confused by this. She tried to allay our fears by explaining how Bristol Oncology Department was a main data link with other worldwide centres and she would now set about gathering as much information as possible. She also elaborated on how Bristol hospital had never before come across such a liver tumour in a child. The most common tumour was categorised as a hepatoblastoma, but Aaron's histology was not a match to this. Leaving the room we were in a daze. I was again angry because of all this bad news, which had so easily extinguished any hope we had previously.

We played the waiting game over the next few days. Austin returned to Taunton and work, and Bernadette went home to Ireland where she would wait to hear news of the next course of treatment. She knew that we were not in a good place with Aaron's diagnosis and she was ready to return as soon as we reached the next stage.

In those weeks the nursing staff were my friends and it was in Carol I found the most strength. She was a pleasantly plump staff nurse who became part of my family. She would fill in any gaps in information, realising how overwhelming it was all becoming for me. I recall her sitting with me many a time, holding my hand, asking what I needed to know, never failing to leave me reassured. She had a devotion to this oncology ward that amazed us, and another like her I have yet to meet. She is indeed one of life's unaccounted but present angels.

Those early weeks were consumed by tests, more scans and searching the internet to gather as much information as possible about this tumour. The hospital became our new home and we became institutionalised. How easy it is, when life demands it of you, to adapt suddenly to scenarios beyond your control, to walk away from all that was your normal mode of living. More importantly, one begins to realise the insignificance and worthlessness of all that you own, and of how priceless it is to hold a child close to you – truly life's greatest gift.

It eventually arrived, that request to meet with Dr Foot in that room again; Carol of course was also present. It was explained to us that there had only been one other recorded histology similar to Aaron's, in Houston, Texas, and that unfortunately that child didn't respond to the chemotherapy protocol. Dr Foot then recommended a course of treatment labelled 'play dough', currently on trial. She felt it was the best and strongest course of action, and of course we agreed, our hopes pinned on the reduction of the tumour followed by surgery.

Aaron would begin his treatment the following week. It was so uplifting to hear that after his treatment he would be allowed home with us and would return for his next course within three weeks. This was, however, the first and last occasion on which I would experience any feeling of joy leaving that room.

Carol prepared us for how the chemo would be administered and the possible side effects. We soon became very learned in the area of oncology, red blood cells, white blood cells, platelet counts, flushing out, mouth ulcers, hair loss, infection, and care when changing Aaron's nappies. This all soon became daily procedure.

In those first days of chemo, Aaron, thank God, was oblivious to what was happening. He sat in his cot as the drip was attached to his line and drop by drop the drugs entered. It took only a short time, and although I sat waiting for some sudden change in him, he just smiled as we played, as if to let me know that it wasn't so bad after all.

CHAPTER IV

—————

A TIME FOR FUN
Being at Home

Following Aaron's first course of treatment we soon adapted to the medical care that was now part of his day-to-day routine. Though initially overwhelmed by all the medical jargon, before long we would automatically follow the procedures, and Dr Foot, along with the nursing staff, explained everything ever so gently and carefully, always reassuring us. It was comforting when each nurse arrived to check on Aaron's administration of chemotherapy; they would describe in detail what was happening and we never felt alienated.

I soon realised that my lack of knowledge surrounding cancer treatment created a fear in me, and I prepared myself for those three days when Aaron would be receiving his chemotherapy. But actually there was nothing other than a sense of calm, with occasional bouts of sadness, as we came to grips with the notion that our journey had really begun and the only hope now was that the liver tumour would shrink in size.

As I mentioned before, the histology of Aaron's tumour was without classification as it didn't have the same cell make-up of a hepatoblastoma, the usual type of liver tumour found in children. Difficulty therefore arose in establishing a specific chemotherapy drug protocol. Professor Mott confirmed that it was one of the rarest liver tumours seen in Bristol Hospital, and there was no other documented case in the UK but research had begun in the US and other countries.

In the meantime, it was recommended that Aaron commence 'play dough'. The drugs would be similar to those administered in adult liver cancer treatment but in smaller doses. We now pinned all our hopes on this.

Two weeks after Aaron's first course of treatment Dr Foot arrived into the ward and asked if we would like to take Aaron home between his treatments as his blood counts were back to normal. I was thrilled with this news for it seemed an eternity since we were all together at home. As soon as she left I immediately rang Austin to tell him and started to pack; there was nowhere else I wanted to be but back home with my two boys and Austin. We would have two weeks there and would return for Aaron's second course of treatment in mid-July.

During this time Aaron was visited every second day by Sarah, the CLIC nurse who would watch his progress and liaise with the hospital and the oncology team (CLIC, meaning Cancer and Leukaemia In Childhood, was founded in 1976 as a charity trust for young cancer patients and their families). We were so grateful for this strong and invaluable source of support both to Aaron and to us as a family. We truly felt minded and never isolated or abandoned with our fears. The care at this time left me feeling as if I had the reassurance and expertise of the ward within my own home. We also felt confident enough to allow Colette, who had arrived over to us a week after Aaron's initial diagnosis, to return to Ireland and resume her life following weeks of caring for Colin and keeping our home running like clockwork.

As I wished friends on the ward a temporary goodbye, I could sense their sharing of our happiness for this small respite. Aaron at this stage was very comfortable with the treatment and experienced few side effects. I was prepared that during these weeks when we would be at home he would lose his beautiful golden hair, but I took it as very small price for what we all hoped would be a successful outcome in the long term. It was just so good driving towards home and then seeing Colin at the window waiting for his brother. He had decorated the lounge with pictures he had drawn to welcome us back. Aaron, I knew, recognised everything and was all smiles as he sat in his bouncer watching TV with Colin.

I now had a different routine, making sure Aaron's medication was correct and administered daily. I still had a sick child who needed care twenty-four hours a day but I soon established what needed to be done and within a few days became more relaxed and adjusted to the changes. That first day at home I received a phone call from Sarah saying that she would visit the following morning and help me with all the unfamiliar procedures.

Colin grew a little jealous when I brought Aaron's cot back into our room, but it was here that all four of us slept for the next three months. Being home meant I could once again take Colin to school, and everyone welcomed Aaron home. I knew by their reaction, however, that they had seen a change in him. Having never been apart from him we hadn't noticed any major change in his appearance, other than the fact that he was paler and, of course, his head was now bare. I remember ever so clearly that Tuesday morning as I sat with him in my arms having a cuddle: I had just bathed him and as I started to comb his hair it just came away in my hands all at once. Though I was prepared for this, when it actually happened it broke my heart. I held him tightly as my tears fell on to his head. I sat him on the chair and I gathered his hair and placed it in a small plastic bag. Aaron looked at me, smiling in bewilderment as I frantically tried to pile it all up together. I smiled at him, telling him I never realised till now just how handsome he really was. Today I sometimes open this bag and grasp his hair in my hands, feeling close to him.

During July, when Colin was on school holidays, we spent our time lazing around. Aaron returned to hospital for his second course of chemo and we, along with Professor Mott and Dr Foot, felt that his stomach had softened a little and that this may have been because the tumour was responding. It was agreed to have a scan following his third treatment towards the end of August.

We lived our lives around the treatments, but normality did seem to be present, though obviously different than before. My mum and dad came in July and we all shared in very special moments with Aaron. We would stroll to the river to see the ducks and take drives around Somerset. Colin was delighted with all the company of family and friends. Aaron loved sitting in the garden watching Austin and Colin playing ball and I can see him laughing joyously as Colin made funny faces for him.

Sarah arrived most days to check Aaron's bloods and I knew she was also keeping an eye on how we were coping with the change to our lives. She would sit with my mum over a cup of tea and, whenever I left the room, I could hear them whispering about how I was not looking after myself.

Bernadette came over again with her husband Philip and their family and we organised for a professional photographer to come and take pictures of Aaron with his cousins and Colin. We sat poor Aaron in all different positions and moved him so much, but he thoroughly enjoyed the hassle and attention. Aaron loved a noisy house full of people; he never reacted strangely to new faces and would get so excited when his cousins would pull him up and down the lounge in his bouncer, the faster the better.

As he took his afternoon naps I would lie on the bed beside him and simply stare at him. I felt his breath on my neck, and even though I knew he was ill I never thought there would come a day when I would lose these times.

Noel, my brother, arrived from Glasgow, and along with Bernadette we all went for a day to Longleat Safari Park. That day was one of the most special we shared with Aaron, and I remember him devouring an ice-cream and amusing us by how he rushed to finish it. As I fed him and tried to keep him clean he never stopped licking, and today I have on my bedside a photograph of him, his mouth covered with ice-cream.

Both Aaron's and Colin's bedrooms were by this stage filled with new toys and gifts. Colin was delighted because for every toy Aaron received in the hospital he would also benefit greatly. He started to look forward to friends visiting his brother, knowing a little present would arrive for him too. Even though he was spoilt in these months it was good to see him feeling important and not forgotten about. I also believed it was good to explain to him about Aaron's illness but to do so gently, trying to gauge how much he could cope with. It was important that he didn't hear bits of information from various sources and become confused or frightened.

Colin grew up so much in those three months and he loved to help in looking after Aaron. When Aaron sat in his bouncer Colin would wrap his blanket around him and tell him how important it was that he didn't catch a cold when his bloods were low; he too grew very accustomed to medical terms.

As a family we soon appreciated and craved the simpler things in life. Both Austin and I now realised how much our outlook and priorities had changed. We never planned ahead and material interests like home improvements or even shopping were replaced with just having a good day with Aaron at home. Today I thank God that for those precious days.

CHAPTER V

DESPERATELY LOVING YOU, DESPERATELY FAILING YOU

Following Aaron's second course of treatment we were ecstatic to hear both Dr Foot and Professor Mott say that his stomach had softened and was not as distended. Both Austin and I worked hard at on keeping a positive attitude, and I felt my many chats with God late at night had paid off.

Even though I was never deeply religious I had started bartering with God, putting up the defence that we were good parents and would never do harm to others. I pleaded to trade places and take any suffering without questioning if Aaron's life was spared. For those few weeks I thought a deal had been struck and I desperately clung to any sign that I was in some way being given an answer.

From the beginning of Aaron's diagnosis we had received numerous bottles of holy water, from Lourdes, Fatima, Medjugorje, Knock, as well as holy medals, relics and cards. Mum arrived with a beautiful statue from the Good Shepherd Convent in Cork, where both of us had worked. This statue of Our Lady was given on loan and had a history of favours being granted and cures for terminal illness. I kept it constantly at Aaron's bedside and each morning would place it against his stomach and lips.

Austin would constantly bless Aaron's forehead with holy water and at times would place some on his stomach. He was much more religious than me and I never once saw him share my anger or lose faith. Often he bore the brunt of my anger when he supported Noel in his defence of God and why this was happening to us. I hoped that God had stopped listening to me and was instead only hearing Austin's loyal pleas and prayers.

During July and Aaron's first two courses of chemotherapy there was a period of acceptance and mental investment in the various procedures. Such a feeling of renewed hope hit us when, after his second course, Aaron's right side and the hard swelling of the tumour seemed to reduce. Results at last and good news after the past six weeks.

Travelling home from the hospital with Aaron in my arms I thanked God over and over again. So content, I promised Aaron that everything would change now for the better and we would have plenty of fun times ahead.

In those first two weeks life was really good, fuelled by great hope and positivity. We noticed how our own health had improved. Austin was exhausted with all his travelling and keeping home life with Colin ticking over, and I had lost a lot of weight, but now we were more relaxed, eating together and getting full nights' sleep.

It was now the second week of August, 1993, and Aaron was due to begin his third chemotherapy session on a Monday. However, the Wednesday before this I began to notice small changes in him – he was more restless and very cranky; nothing, not even Colin's many attempts to amuse him, seemed to work. He was only content when I rocked him or walked him up and down the lounge. Sarah had been with us the previous day and all appeared to be well, so I felt that maybe he would settle in a matter of time. However, three hours later I was still rocking him and if I tried to lay him down he got more agitated. His screams became more piercing and it seemed as if he was in the same pain he was in that first evening. I decided to ring the nursing staff on the ward and they said it would be best to return to the hospital.

I left Colin with a neighbour, and all the while as I packed Aaron's bag he was becoming more and more distressed and I more and more panicked. I knew it would be a good hour before Austin would be home so I telephoned him to go straight to Bristol to save us time and I would leave with Aaron and drive myself. Austin urged me to wait for him but I couldn't bear the thoughts of Aaron being in pain.

I left to travel to Bristol up the back roads rather than the M5 motorway. Aaron was very uncomfortable in the car seat and he was wriggling his body as if the strap across his stomach was exerting too much pressure for him to bear. As I drove, way too fast, I kept looking at him in the mirror telling him I would soon have him better. I cried as I begged God to ease his pain. Bristol seemed an eternity away. Just as I approached the back road of Bristol Airport a police car followed me and signalled for me to pull over. I wound the window down and the young policeman was met with my hysterical cries and Aaron screaming in the back. In between my broken sobs I explained where I was going, and he wanted to call an ambulance, but I told him it would waste time and that Aaron needed his morphine. He provided us with a police escort to the hospital and we arrived there quickly. I am today in his debt for this understanding and sympathy when I was so distressed.

Carol was awaiting our arrival, and as soon as we did Dr Foot was called and was examining Aaron within minutes. I stood beside her, breathless from rushing, as she felt Aaron's stomach, an intense expression on her face. Carol tried desperately to calm me down but I just kept asking what was wrong. Dr Foot explained that Aaron's stomach was again quite swollen and what they needed to do first of all was to relax the muscles and make him comfortable. She would speak with Professor Mott and return later to have a talk with us.

Within an hour Aaron was sleeping peacefully and I was more relaxed, but still with a nervous, sickly knot in my stomach. When Austin arrived I just burst into tears, saying I just knew something was seriously wrong. Both he and Carol tried to comfort me, but I was so agitated, and I felt that I was being treated like a little girl. I noticed familiar faces of other parents looking into the room as they passed by but I barely made eye contact. While we waited for Dr Foot to return I kept telling Austin how I was just so sick of it all and how I couldn't bear any more bad news. I then telephoned Bernadette to tell her we were back in Bristol. Within a few hours she was on a flight to be with us.

Aaron was comfortable but a lot more dazed, and Carol assured me it was because of the drug used to relax his muscle spasms. I then noticed Dr Foot at the nurses' desk along with Professor Mott, and as they walked towards our cubicle door I knew they were coming with bad news. Professor Mott brought his much welcomed sense of calmness to the room, but even this couldn't ease our biggest fears. As he examined Aaron and played with him I stared intensely at his face. He then sat us both down and explained that Aaron's tumour appeared to have returned to the size it was before treatment, if not bigger. He would have confirmation of this when he saw the scan the following morning. He patted my hand as he urged us just to wait and see. I kept telling myself to accept what he was saying, but as much as I tried I couldn't hold back the tears.

Austin too shared in my anguish but agreed with Professor Mott that we would have to wait for the scan results. He still had a strong sense of hope, and what a wonderful attribute this was and is. This strength kept us going through every stage of Aaron's illness. In retrospect, because we both travelled our journey at different stages, and although conflict arose at times, this allowed us to be at different levels; when one was weak the other grew strong, and it was during these times we held each other most.

Bernadette arrived back to the ward that evening and I could see her chatting with Carol at the nurses' desk. I searched, as I had done on that first night at Musgrove Hospital, for positive body language, but I couldn't catch a single glimpse to show me that they were engaged in light-hearted conversation. As Bernadette made her way to our cubicle she was visibly shaken, but as soon as she entered the room a forced smile surfaced, trying to reassure me that everything was going to be alright.

Aaron had his scan early on Thursday morning and was still very comfortable. His appetite, however, wasn't so good and he now struggled with the bottles he had once swallowed down so quickly. We were all very restless as we waited for the results, and I walked around the ward speaking with other parents and playing with the other children.

Bernadette would pop out for a cigarette with Austin, and when he would arrive back I would go and join her. Together we would sit on that wooden bench outside the main door, watching the world go by, trying to think positively, occasionally discussing the difficulties experienced by other parents on the ward and how they had struggled to cope but had succeeded.

On one occasion when I returned to the ward I found Dr Foot talking with Austin, with Carol by his side looking so sad. As I approached them Dr Foot asked if both myself and Austin would come to the office, that room which I detested so much. Bernadette sat with Aaron and smiled nervously as we left. If I close my eyes today I can so easily return to that room; even the atmosphere I can still sense, and I can replay every moment as Dr Foot sat us both down and pulled her chair towards mine so she could hold my hand. As she began to speak I couldn't look at her; instead my eyes roved the room, avoiding any acknowledgement that she was trying to comfort me. She described how the scan had shown that Aaron's tumour hadn't responded to the chemotherapy and in fact had continued to grow. It was also clearly evident that the mass hadn't originated on any particular lobe of the liver but in the centre, so even if treatment had shrunk it, surgery wouldn't have been on option either. She also revealed that there appeared to be secondaries in Aaron's lungs as well as a deposit in his heart. I questioned what his chances of survival were and asked her to give me a percentage. Looking back, it was so ridiculous, but I started throwing out numbers like 50 per cent, 40, 20, and when I got to 10 per cent she nodded and said 'less than'.

Austin and I clung to each other, crying, not wanting to believe this awful outcome. Every one of our hopes was destroyed. Dr Foot left us for a while as we tried to accept that it was all over. We returned to Bernadette who was sitting holding Aaron. Totally distraught, we rubbed Aaron's face, wiping away our tears. Carol joined us, her sadness clearly evident as she tried to console us. We knew now that Aaron had only a very short time, weeks, and that he would not be returning home. That day I returned to CLIC House and directed a tirade at those in the kitchen when I couldn't find Aaron's yoghurts, at those who had been my crutch, but still they comforted me, knowing our news was not good.

In the days that followed I grew restless with the hospital routine and annoyed that I wasn't doing enough for Aaron. I questioned every day what we were doing sitting around just waiting for him to die. The guilt of failing him was killing me. Noel arrived to a torrent of abuse about God, and every time the hospital chaplain came to bless Aaron I ignored his prayers and his comforting. My anger was an anger he knew so well, but never did he fail in his daily visits and kind words to Aaron, who accepted him with a smile.

I became so intolerant of the days passing and nothing constructive being done to help our boy. One afternoon I decided that I had had enough and I told Austin I wanted second opinions on Aaron's prognosis. It meant so much to me to just keep on trying. Aaron deserved parents who wouldn't give up, and I could never rest knowing that I sat and wondered but never travelled to gather any more information. I decided I wanted to go to Great Ormond Street. From the very first time I heard of Aaron's diagnosis that hospital had been in my mind. I had heard of its reputation, of its fantastic work, sometimes against all the odds. I also wanted to see a liver specialist rather than an oncologist to get more information, but most of all I wanted Aaron to know how desperately we struggled to keep him with us.

Dr Foot understood our heartbreak and arranged for us to see Dr John Pitchard in Great Ormond Street and Mr Casey Tan in King's Hospital. We travelled to London with Aaron, Austin driving and I holding on to him tightly in the back. I now noticed how ill Aaron looked, especially in the daylight, out of the fluorescent lighting of the hospital ward.

We met with Dr Pitchard, the oncology paediatric consultant. He was a lot younger than I had expected, and without that typical conservative consultant's disposition. I remember thinking how casually dressed he was, in cord trousers and check shirt, but so natural and warm-hearted. He studied the scans and medical information Dr Foot had given him, pointing to and explaining different details as he did so. He spoke also of the rarity of Aaron's tumour and the fact that it was the first of its kind he had seen. He was direct but compassionate, and he understood our search for various opinions. But he too supported the prognosis of Bristol and wished us luck with our meeting that afternoon in King's Hospital.

Mr Casey Tan was a liver transplant surgeon. He sat with us and explained how because of Aaron's secondaries it would be impossible to consider him for a liver transplant. That day we returned to Bristol with Aaron, tired and emotionally exhausted, feeling that we had utterly failed him.

Within a few days I again started going on overdrive and decided to contact Sloan-Kettering Clinic in New York. Dr O'Reilly, chief of paediatrics, had agreed to study Aaron's case and showed much interest in it. I urged Dr Foot to forward some slide tissues and scans to Dr O'Reilly, as he had requested, and it was at this point that I had my first confrontation with her. She was reluctant initially to follow my request and release the slides, but following days of pestering of both herself and Dr Mott she finally relented. Within a week I received information from Sloan-Kettering stating that if 30 per cent of the liver was free of tumour, regardless of secondaries, they would operate. I, of course, became obsessed with wanting to take Aaron to Sloan-Kettering. Austin was cautious but too afraid to disagree with my need to do this for Aaron. I spoke with Dr Foot and she pleaded with me not to do this to Aaron and ourselves. She felt Aaron was too ill and wouldn't survive, and his quality of life while undergoing procedures would be unbearable and unfair to him. She went into considerable detail as to what would be involved and insisted that the end result would be very traumatic for Aaron and that the treatment would leave him without dignity.

I felt like I was abandoning Aaron to this disease, but I knew Dr Foot was right, and the word 'dignity' stayed to the forefront of my mind. All through his diagnosis and chemotherapy treatments, dignity was Aaron's main attribute: he showed dignity, he earned dignity and it was this sense of dignity that he needed to leave with most of all.

Those next few weeks we spent every hour loving him, crying with him, laughing with him, just being with him as we slowly lost him.

Those who knew him came and shared their special time with him, every visit an honour and a treasured memory.

REMEMBERING MICHAEL – WITH A MILLION LOVE SONGS

Those three months on the oncology ward left me with a new found knowledge of what the true values in life are, and I thank God that enabled me in the following years and troubled times to ground myself. My pain was a pain endured by other parents, and even though it was unbearable for us at times I am today so grateful for the abundant supply of emotional love and support that cushioned me when things got too much. This was brought home to me when I saw what a difficult and lonely struggle it was for one remarkable mother whose twelve-year-old son battled leukaemia. Bernadette had struck up a friendship with Michael's mum, Elizabeth. She was a warm, natural lady, separated, coping on her own with her only son's illness.

My first encounter with Michael was in the kitchen as I prepared food for Aaron. He burst though the door introduced himself and immediately starting asking questions about us and Aaron and why we were here. He was fascinated by the strong Irish accent and had great fun trying to imitate me. He was a constant talker and had that wonderful ability to change the atmosphere by his mere presence. Michael was a handsome young boy with beautiful brown eyes, and when he smiled, those gorgeous dimples came to life. He was, of course, ill and receiving treatment but he had retained some hair, of which he was mighty proud. During our three months I became close to this young 'laddy', as I called him. We would spend many an afternoon discussing films and TV programmes, playing cards, or he would simply accompany me and Aaron on our daily tour around the hospital. Every morning, first thing on his way to the shower, he would knock at the window and blow Aaron a kiss. He would return all clean and smelling so nice. I would tell him how much 'hunkier' he was getting by the day. He would blush, and I can still see him peeking cheekily from beneath his baseball cap. His mum adored him and the love oozed between them; indeed, he was ahead of his years in the way he protected her and openly displayed affection for her.

One evening as I sat outside with his mum, she spoke of how Michael's illness was a constant race of trying to keep one step ahead all the time, how hope would engulf her when he was in remission, but despair would soon take over when this grace period ended. I could see the fear she had of losing him, and how all these pressures had taken their toll on her physically. She looked so tired and worn out, with dark circles around her eyes, but when Michael appeared she would just light up. I never thought anybody could be in a worse position than us, but to watch her cope without the emotional support and love of a partner was, I felt, unbearably difficult.

Michael was also my 'personal assistant', a title that amused him so much. When I would leave Aaron for a few moments he would sit with him. Whenever I needed a nurse he would frantically search the ward and always return with one. When Aaron and I had visitors he would arrive in, and all those who were privileged to meet him thoroughly enjoyed his company. He, without a doubt, brought sunshine to a world of darkness. But in Aaron's final days I lost contact with Michael, and in the weeks that followed I became swallowed up in my own loss and grief.

I had vowed the day I left Bristol never to return again. However, two months after Aaron died I received a letter from Michael's mum. She sympathised with the loss of Aaron and spoke about how she was now back in Bristol after a brief spell at home and of how Michael was not doing so good. Yet, true to his character he was battling with all he had. She wrote of how she remembered my family and thanked me for the kindness shown to them both. Today I am still in awe of how she, in the midst of her own pain, reached out to me with amazing empathy, knowing it would be a road she would soon travel. I often question if indeed I could have faced this knowledge and fear with such dignity. Her suffering was palpable, and though I tried desperately to take flight from a place that filled me with fear, I knew I had to return to see my young 'laddy'. I felt it would be unfair to ask Austin to come along, so one morning I just decided to get up and go. I bought Michael a new cap, a discman and Take That's latest album. I drove to Bristol, up the back country roads, reliving my last journey with Aaron. I would instinctively glance now and then in the rear-view mirror, but now there was no baby's car seat. What amazed me was not Aaron's absence but the strong sense of his presence. This, I felt, was his way of telling me I had made the right decision and he was alongside me, comforting me. As I came closer to Bristol the lump in my throat grew bigger, especially as I pulled up outside the hospital. I noticed new parents huddled outside, now locked into the world of childhood illness. I sat for what seemed an eternity with that awful knot in my stomach, so desperately wanting to see Michael without having to go back inside. But I knew that that was no deal.

I arrived up into the ward, heart racing, a crumbled heap deep inside, but trying hard to look calm and composed. As I passed the room where Aaron died I gave a quick glance and saw new toys and a little girl of about three years lying in bed, her parents by her side. I expected to feel intense sadness but was surprised by the overwhelming sense of relief that my beautiful son was no longer there. Then I was startled when I noticed a photo of Aaron on Carol's board, or as I had once angrily and unjustifiably christened it, the RIP board. I know there are so many success stories and photos of now healthy children there also. However, there was my little man smiling at me as if to tell me that all was just fine. I was deep in thought when I heard Carol's familiar voice and felt her arms around me. Michael had been transferred to another floor and as we went to him Carol explained that he was not good and that his mum had been devastated when his treatment was stopped.

Michael had indeed deteriorated but his eyes still had that wonderful mischievous sparkle. This lovely young man who was once so talkative was now tired and pale. While I was visiting, his mum went to CLIC House for a break, and I will forever be grateful for and cherish my special time alone with my young 'laddy'. Despite his apparent lack of energy he was so thankful for the gifts and we played his favourite track on the discman, 'A Million Love Songs', his faded but angelic Welsh voice singing along word for word. He smiled as I teased him that no one in the band had his good looks. These days, when I hear that song, Michael stands alongside me, humming softly. I take such great comfort in knowing that Aaron now has my wonderful personal assistant to look after him.

And for that, dear Michael, I thank you with a million love songs. It was an honour, my young laddy, to have been in the presence of such a wonderful young man.

CHAPTER VI

—◦◦◦—

ON THE WINGS OF BUTTERFLIES

For over an hour I cradled Aaron in my arms. I held his tiny hands in mine, desperately trying to rub them warm. I wanted just to stay in this moment for ever, and willed time to stand still and let us be. It was now all over; those tidal waves of chaos that had churned us about in the past three months had finally subsided and left us with a sense of calmness so alien and difficult to be with. Even as coldness crept into his soft skin, that baby smell remained, and how I craved every sense of him as my nose settled upon his forehead. Words wouldn't come as I looked to Noel and Bernadette, who were visibly heart-broken. Austin wept as he urged me to let go of Aaron. This moment was for me the most difficult of all. It was at this point that Dr Ramaille came and knelt beside me and uttered those words about how some day good would come from our grief.

We had agreed to an autopsy whereby Aaron's tumour would be removed for research. It was a request made to us two weeks before his death, and extremely difficult for us as parents. Both Austin and I struggled as we differed in our beliefs; Austin begged me to let Aaron be, but following Professor Mott's plea of how important it was to study this particular tumour, I persuaded Austin, after hours of tears and anguish, to give his consent so that we could in some way help the next poor parents. Today I know how much signing the consent form broke his heart, and for this alone I will love him for ever.

Dr Ramaille slowly released my grip, finger by finger, his eyes locked with mine and sharing my tears. It was then I noticed that Carol was also in the room. She came and took

Aaron from me, still speaking to him, and she lovingly placed him in his cot, telling him how handsome we would now make him. For the very last time I washed him, changed his nappy, applied baby powder and dressed him in his navy striped t-shirt, yellow shorts and socks. I bent to kiss his lips and then placed his soother in his mouth. For the first time I recognised that Aaron was now at peace and the pain he had so bravely borne was no longer punishing his tiny body. Austin carried him in his arms as we went to the hospital chapel. It truly amazed me that so many people passed by not knowing that Aaron was no longer with us. I remember thinking how, even in the presence of death, life will not be taken hostage.

The chapel was a small room, bright and welcoming. In the corner was a small square bed and it was into this that we placed Aaron. We sat around him, Bernadette rubbing his tiny hands, only stopping to wipe away her tears. Noel gently caressed Aaron's cheeks and blessed his forehead. He then looked at me and asked if I was okay. I turned my head away from him, so angry with his God that I failed to recognise the loving brother he was to me.

In the chapel was a book of condolences filled with heartbreaking words from those parents who had been here before us. We wrote our own private thoughts and in a way it helped me close Aaron's time in Bristol hospital. An hour later it was time for Aaron's autopsy and we kissed him goodbye for a while. This was so difficult for Austin that he completely broke down. I panicked, wondering if I had made the right decision, but in my heart I knew that no parents deserved to be where we were at that moment. All those in the medical field work tirelessly to search for a cure, and this I witnessed first-hand at Bristol Hospital for Sick Children. It was now our time to give something back.

Austin and I decided to return to Taunton to collect Colin from school and break the news to him. Bernadette promised to stay and wait for Aaron, as it was so important to me that he was not on his own. We left the hospital with Noel and walked towards CLIC House. Everything felt numb and surreal. We walked in silence and bewilderment, as if we were the only survivors of some horrific trauma. This silence was suddenly broken by Noel collapsing and breaking down in tears. I rushed back to hold him up as he fell against the wall uttering the words 'Oh how I loved him' over and over again. Noel, who had been a remarkable tower of strength, held by such amazing faith, had succumbed to the injustice of it all. For those few moments I came to recognise that even those with the most intense of faith are also tested. What courage it takes to bear this pain and accept God's will without questioning. I had over those past three months ridiculed Noel about his God, a god who turned away from hearing my pleas of desperation. I recall vividly one particular day when Noel was very much in the firing line. The previous night Aaron, who at this point had been attached to a morphine pump, was very distressed and uncomfortable. I begged the night doctor to increase the dosage as he waited for Dr Foot to arrive and sign her consent. She had been attending a medical dinner and when contacted had made her way back to the oncology ward. For those thirty minutes I paced up and down the room begging God to ease Aaron's suffering. It was on that night I abandoned my God and the next day I had let Noel know as much. To take my son was something I would have to cope with, but to leave him in pain I couldn't accept. Now I saw Noel pinned by grief against the wall, but still loyal to his faith. It was this same faith that had enabled him to support us when we were at our lowest.

Aaron had passed away on a Friday afternoon and Noel knew how difficult it would be to have his body released for burial back in Ireland. However, he also knew what this meant to us and he did not fail us.

Austin and I arrived back in Taunton to collect Colin. I felt so physically sick at the thought of having to tell him – what words would I use? – that I had to get Austin to pull over. The principal of the school met us at the door and expressed sympathy on behalf of the staff. Colin came from class and as we travelled home I told him that his baby brother had gone to heaven. At first he listened and simply nodded, and then I noticed the tears silently streaming down his young face. He was just a baby himself, and the only brother he would ever have was now gone.

We arrived back at the house to a heartbroken Colette, who had kept our house a home for Colin. She had taken leave of absence from work and put her life on hold without once questioning for how long. She was indeed in the most lonely and difficult of places, trying to establish some sort of normality for Colin and wanting so much to be with us and Aaron in Bristol. The house had taken on an eerie silence. I walked around searching for any reminders of Aaron and spotted some empty bottles and his medicine tray on the kitchen counter top. Colette had ironed clothes belonging to Aaron and placed them on the dining-room table. I took a vest of his, clutched it in my hands and smothered myself in his smell, a smell I would hunger for and feed in years to come.

I telephoned my parents back in Cork, knowing how distraught they were. My father answered and he ever so gently tried to comfort me and ease my pain with words full of love and concern. My mother's voice, however, was void of his strength and failed to remain composed, and her trembling wouldn't allow clear words to surface. But words were not necessary now. We both knew, though apart, that we were all locked into a world of despair. As grandparents, it was not a loss they should have borne witness to. After speaking with them I went to my bedroom, where Aaron's cot still stood beside our bed, his music mobile still hanging over his pillow. I pulled the cord and listened to his favourite tune and remembered how I would hum it to him as he slept beside me. All I wanted was my little boy back.

Noel had by this stage managed to arrange our flights home to Cork with Aaron for Sunday evening. Luckily the funeral directors in Taunton would have a coffin ready in time. Bernadette suggested she travel from the hospital by car holding Aaron in her arms and she asked me for that special moment with him. I struggled with this at first but I knew how important it was to her, the last time they would spend together. Two hours later as we sat in the funeral home my darling Aaron arrived cradled in her arms. As I snuggled him into me Bernadette looked at him, smiled and whispered into his ear, 'I see you're back young man, you had a right laugh at me'. She explained that for the whole journey he was never in her arms. She felt that his presence and his spirit had left with Austin and myself when we went for Colin, and as soon as he entered my arms she saw him return. She said that it was his mother he always wanted to be with and whom he never left. Today those words are so true – he has not for one day ever left me.

We spent that evening with Aaron. My friend Jane and Dr Scanlon joined us for a time and occasionally we smiled at the fact that we were all still whispering and I was still rocking him as though he were asleep. We sat with Aaron until early evening and then the funeral directors explained that they needed time with him; they showed such amazing kindness and compassion, reassuring us that we could return at any time no matter how late.

Leaving Aaron behind with unfamiliar people tore me to pieces. I felt that yet again I was failing him as his mother, such was the overwhelming sense of my abandonment. That very first evening at home without Aaron was just a blur. I vaguely remember sitting with friends and neighbours around the dining room table drinking tea, as Bernadette and Colette scurried around making salads and sandwiches. Occasionally out of the corner of my eye I would catch them whispering to a friend about how I was coping, and they tried to get me to eat just a little. Sitting there I now knew what an out-of-body experience was like – I felt completely numb and detached. At times I became so agitated with the small talk, though I knew friends' intentions were full of kindness, as they tried their best to care for me and make things normal. But I didn't want to go back to normality –

how could I? Normal was to have Aaron sitting in my arms, but nobody could arrange that. I would watch Austin trying hard to make conversation though I knew he too wasn't really there. He had such a sad emptiness in his eyes.

Later that evening Noel accompanied us back to Aaron. Our little boy seemed colder but so peaceful, and I remember thinking that this was his first uninterrupted sleep in a long while and he looked as if he were enjoying it. On Saturday evening we gathered with friends for a special Mass. I was so touched by all those who came to say their goodbyes to Aaron before his final journey back to Cork.

I became very emotional when Carol and the nursing staff also said their farewells. Children from Colin's school had made lovely flower arrangements and the church altar was decorated in a harvest theme with baskets of fruits and vegetables. Noel spoke with such warmth and yet was so composed. As Aaron's uncle it must have been so hard for him to deliver such a dignified and yet emotional service. One hour later Austin carried Aaron in his arms, a father and his son sharing this special but heartbreaking moment. Walking behind, squeezing Colin's little hand in mine, I suddenly noticed two beautifully coloured butterflies fluttering around Aaron's tiny white coffin, creating a wonderful atmosphere of peace and tranquillity. When Austin stopped at the end doors the butterflies flew high into the sky. This was an amazing salute to our darling Aaron.

As we made our way to Heathrow Airport, Aaron was placed in the front seat of the hearse, while Austin and I, along with Colin, Bernadette and Colette, sat just behind. Every now and then we would tenderly run our fingers across his coffin, still longing to touch him. During those three hours Colette and Bernadette reminisced about their own childhood, and we laughed as we recalled funny incidents. Looking back now, I believe this was some sort of emotional hysteria, a way of clinging to each other, holding on to the pieces of our broken hearts.

As our flight arrived into Cork, Aaron was indeed back home. It was a wet, misty, dark evening and as we approached the terminal we were met by my brother Charlie, who just opened his arms as he walked towards us. I was completely taken aback when we entered the arrivals hall, for there were so many friends and family gathered to support us. I became overwhelmed as people surrounded me offering words of comfort. I then noticed my father standing alongside my mother hugging Colette and Bernadette. Those swollen red eyes and tired ashen face will remain with me forever. Our eyes locked as he smiled over at me and I quickly went to him and wrapped myself within his large frame. For those few moments I was again just his little girl, feeling so safe, knowing he could always make things a little better.

Aaron was given a special Garda escort to Wilton funeral home. Here we opened his coffin and family and friends said their goodbyes. For some it was their first and final meeting with Aaron. Nothing, however, prepared me for our own private kisses goodbye. I talked and talked to him, telling him how I loved him and would some day hold him once more. All I wanted at that moment was to sweep him up in my arms, take him home to my bed and cuddle him until my own very last day when I could also go with him. I kept slowly moving back to allow friends and family their final time with him, but I would frantically return for one more touch, making sure his soother was okay and his teddy was snuggled beside him. I kept fixing him as if he were asleep in his cot, trying to keep him cosy and warm beneath the white silk covering.

The following morning Aaron was received into the SMA church in Wilton. Here again Noel wonderfully brought Aaron's personality alive, relaying how he had touched all those who shared in his short time with us. Our time was now coming to an end and Austin stepped out once more to gather Aaron in his arms. Following behind him, as I raised my tear-filled eyes, two butterflies once again fluttered over Aaron and for just a short few moments I felt my little boy tenderly comforting me.

CHAPTER VII

A Place for You to Sleep

Our darling Aaron was laid to rest in St Oliver's cemetery, Cork city. We chose St Oliver's because it meant so much to me that Aaron would now be in the caring bosom of my family. Returning him home to where my own heart will always be gave me such great comfort. St Oliver's is within a ten minute drive of my sister Bernadette's home and here he would be looked after.

Those two weeks following Aaron's death are the most difficult for me to remember. Today I have very fragmented memories and I struggle to recall how I passed this time.

Food I ate I took no pleasure from, people I sat with I couldn't see or hear, places I went to all looked the same, but I do remember oftentimes standing in the shower in the morning, the water running down my face and mixing with my tears, tears at the thought of passing through another day like this, without Aaron, and feeling that even if I'd been the victim of some horrific attack I could not have felt a pain worse than this, the pain of a heart torn apart. I often feel riddled with guilt that I wasn't present as a mother for Colin at this time. I still had a son, I could see him and touch him, but my hunger for Aaron was overwhelming. I had one purpose each day and that was just, every morning, to go to his grave.

I was now desperate to be beside him, quite content to replace sitting by his hospital bed with lying on his grave. Still wanting to comfort him and to let him know I was there.

During those two weeks it tore me apart when it rained, especially at night. I would panic, thinking of how cold and wet and alone he was. One night I slipped from bed, put a coat on over my nightdress and went to him. Even the eeriness of a graveyard in the dead of night brought no fear, I craved my son so much. I wanted to push my hands through the earth to him and bring him back with me to my bed, and leaving the graveyard I turned my head several times, such was the awful sense of abandonment I felt.

I hated God so much for taking my son, and anger began to consume me slowly. I became hostile towards those around me. Even simple setbacks made me annoyed, and I wanted nothing to do with family and friends. I withdrew from Austin, Colin and those who supported me so much, and all I wanted was to be left alone, not constantly watched and being asked how I was.

Aaron's death had ripped through the lives and hearts of all my family, and the fall-out was evident. My parents' faces were etched with pain and tiredness, and I could barely look at them or sit in their presence; exhaustion was also visible on my sisters' faces, burnt out from this unbearable grief. A family that was so close was now at times so distant, each in their own worlds desperately holding their own sense of loss.

After the emotionally charged months of total upheaveal, we now had to go back to living our lives, but we were so unprepared for this. Even the simplest of things like an uninterrupted night's sleep, after being so used to the sounds of a busy hospital ward, was hard to get used to. For weeks my body clock was in total chaos, still locked into hospital time. Awake 5.30 every morning, but now silence replaced the busy sounds of the hospital ward. I even found it difficult to sleep on a bed, so used had my body become to lying on the floor or sitting upright on a chair for hours on end. It was more difficult to return to normality than leave it without warning.

The day arrived when we had to leave Cork and return to our lives in Taunton. Colin needed to go back to school, see his friends and maybe now have the security of his mum and dad being there for him. Leaving Aaron's grave that Sunday morning, knowing it would be weeks before I would return, I removed the flowers that had now wilted and carefully placed his two favourite teddies on the earth that was still so fresh. I had dreaded this day. But, for the first time, I didn't look back as I walked towards the gate. I was not leaving you, darling Aaron, for you came with me. There was no need to say our goodbyes: the strong sense of your presence would not allow it.

CHAPTER VIII

RETURNING WITHOUT YOU

We returned to our house in Taunton on 16 October 1993. I call it our house because it was no longer a home without our youngest son. I remember thinking back to the first day we received the keys and how happy we were to begin settling in a new neighbourhood, but that day as I walked into this house I felt nothing but contempt and anger.

Over the next few months I was haunted day and night by the memories enclosed in its walls. I wasn't prepared for the unbearable loneliness. I wanted to give Colin back even a simple and basic routine, which he deserved from a mother who had become so immersed in a world of grief that she had abandoned him. Austin had taken leave from work to be with me during those critical weeks, and each morning when he would take Colin to school, I would wave them goodbye with a pretence of a smile, but as soon as the car left the drive I would crumple into a heap, grasping Aaron's t-shirt in my hands, sniffing and craving him.

Thank God that during that time when I was so weak Austin was so strong, for I could not have borne the pain of both of us. Today, Austin, I thank you for this from the bottom of my heart. If we both had dissolved together I dread to think how we could have journeyed back.

How my dearest friends Cherry and Jane tolerated me when I returned to Taunton; how I tested our friendships and pushed all the boundaries. Never once did they isolate me but together they held my hand and walked me out of my grief. Sometimes when they visited I wouldn't ever get out of bed and they would sit for hours relaying all the gossip and waiting patiently for some interested reaction. They understood my grief with an abundance of sympathy and compassion.

Time waits for no one and it certainly had no intention of waiting for me. Little by little as the weeks passed by I slowly emerged from this world of hiding. Every day brought its own challenges and situations, some of which I was prepared for, but it was the unexpected incidences that pushed me at times on to a rollercoaster of emotional chaos.

I appreciated that different people dealt with the death of a child in different ways, but at times I felt so confused and isolated by reactions from neighbours, especially when they avoided me. One morning I decided to walk alone along the canal that myself and Aaron had often travelled. I had heard that while we were in Bristol a neighbour whom I had often stopped and chatted with had had twins. I noticed her walking towards me with her new baby boys, but as she caught my gaze she turned quickly to avoid me. Deep down I knew it was she who had difficulty with my pain but it tore me apart.

Trips to the supermarket when I would automatically go straight for the baby aisle would leave me in a state of panic, and I would rush back to my car. There were mornings when I received sample Pampers nappies for the next stage that Aaron would have been at; teddy bear picnic invitations held by the local hospital that I had months previously signed up for would be waiting for me on the hall floor. Every day something to remind me of how our lives should have been, mornings when I would wake thinking it would be a good day and then would spend most of it in tears. Years later when I began to train as a psychotherapist I learnt that these were the normal stages of a grieving process, and that I had to go through all the stages. Even today the end has yet to arrive, but nor do I want it to: this pain is entitled to be with you. No matter how you try to escape it, it accompanies you for life.

Six months after Aaron died we returned to Ireland. Austin moved companies to Manor Foods, Co. Cavan, and we decided to live in Dublin. I was so happy to come home, and within a year our daughter Chloe was born. My pregnancy went very well physically, but emotionally it was extremely difficult. I had felt the void in Colin's life in not having a sibling and I desperately wanted to fill that loneliness. When Chloe was born I was constantly worrying and terrified when she wasn't well, forever checking her skin colour, feeling her stomach and insisting on liver scans. The constant reassurance from specialists that the chances of Aaron's cancer being genetic was a million to one brought me no comfort for I had won that lottery before. When Chloe reached the age of two I relaxed more, and normal life resumed again.

In the years that followed I returned to college and trained as a beauty therapist and then worked with the cosmetic company Elizabeth Arden, but I always felt I had something special to share with other parents who would travel the journey of childhood cancer. I would for the next six years keep in contact with Carol, and my ties to Bristol were never severed. In my mind I easily returned to CLIC House and travelled to each room, visualising parents struggling to come to terms with their child's diagnosis. Time doesn't excuse the pain but what it does guarantee is, if you are lucky enough, a day of acceptance. For some, holding on to anger blocks its path. It took eight years for my own day of acceptance to arrive, when I was no longer hostage to bitterness and anger, when I could walk into a church and say to God, 'OK, you have him for a while, but I know each day that passes is a day closer to when I can hold him once more'. I stopped the torment of questioning why, replacing it with a sense that maybe it was because we were strong enough to bear it. I could very easily have lived a life of moving on, placing our experience as a family into the memory box of Aaron's toys and clothes that today still stands at the foot of my bed. However, I started to question whether it was acceptable merely to store Aaron away as a memory; did he not bestow on us something a lot more powerful? I knew how special he was and how lucky we were to have had him amongst us.

To walk away would have been easier, but I was constantly uneasy about withholding what I could share with other parents. In 2002 I decided to return to college for four years to train as a psychotherapist and to specialise in bereavement counselling. I began my own journey in personal therapy, which was my own healing process. During those four years I also gave birth to a second daughter, Ava, a complete surprise, but what joy she has brought to us. My life has become so enriched from my work and through it I have the wonderful honour of helping those who now face the trauma of grief and loss.

CHAPTER IX

―――∞∞∞―――

'CLIC'. Had I ever understood what this abbreviation represented before Aaron's illness? No! Was it a word my family was familiar with? No! Did I ever even acknowledge its existence when I tossed a few pence into the box on flag days? No!

Prior to Aaron's diagnosis cancer was a disease that only entered the lives of other families, families I hadn't even a distant connection to. It was a disease I mainly associated with adults and something I can only remember my parents referring to as 'the big C'.

As a mother, my own fears of childhood illness had been limited to the common aliments like colic, croup, chest infections, tummy bugs, measles and chicken pox, and the one I had dreaded most of all, meningitis. All those I had knowledge of, so in some way I was prepared and equipped in the event of their occurance. However, not for one minute, even in those quiet, still moments of the night when my motherly worries about my children became pronounced, did I once consider cancer.

I soon found out that no matter how distant you feel from this disease, it has the ability to creep into your world purely at random. As a parent of a terminally ill child, you are consumed twenty-four hours a day with the agonising thoughts of what you could have done to prevent this, and indeed this is the most soul-destroying pain that it leaves.

Nothing seems so unjust as serious illness in a child. Any parent would willingly give up their own life to save their child's. How I had begged God so often, first with pleas and then with anger, to let me bear this disease. I had tormented myself with questions of what Aaron had done to deserve this. He was pure, without sin, an angel who just brought joy and happiness, a gift from a God who just wanted him back. We were still locked into our own world of shock and disbelief, and in that place I would never find an understanding. It was to come when as a family we first entered through the doors of CLIC House, for it was here that we soon found out we were not so unique and we were not alone – we were simply just another normal family amongst so many embarking on this journey.

It was on our first weekend in Bristol that I heard parents say how they were staying in this house during their child's treatment. All spoke of the wonderful support this facility gave them, both practically and, more importantly, emotionally.

Those first few days and nights Bernadette, Austin and I never left Aaron's side. We slept on mattresses provided and I sat on a pink leather armchair by his cot where I could wrap his little fingers in mine as he slept.

It was on the Monday morning that the hospital social worker arrived and ever so gently encouraged us to avail of the facilities provided by CLIC House, both for ourselves and for family members who would travel from Cork to be with Aaron. Aware that our initial period in the hospital would be a matter of weeks rather than days she voiced her concern about the physical and emotional exhaustion that would creep upon us as a family and how it must be a priority to take care of ourselves also at this time.

She emphasised that CLIC House would help us to cope with even the practical necessities such as showering, laundry and cooking healthy meals, allowing us to retain the strength to focus on Aaron. It would also relieve the financial burden. That Monday morning I listened and thanked her, and she smiled warmly as I politely explained to her that I had no intention of ever leaving Aaron's side, let alone sleep away from him for a night.

In retrospect I was, of course, oblivious to the long road ahead, and she, in turn, was all too familiar with this initial reaction. It was a smile of compassionate acknowledgement, and she would return within the next few days and coax me to this wonderful house that became our home from home.

The story of how CLIC came to be is borne out of a personal tragedy. A tragedy that saw the young son of an entrepreneurial Bristol builder and property developer, Bob Woodward, develop a rare cancer of the nervous system. Robert Woodward was just eight years old in 1974 when he was diagnosed with neuroblastoma. Sadly Robert didn't survive but he left behind a wonderful legacy. Founded by Robert's father, the charity CLIC has placed cancer in childhood on the public agenda and has led to developments in the field of research, as well as financial support for the medical services and welfare programme.

In conjunction with Professor Mott, Bob Woodward created good from despair. He saw first-hand how parents struggled to cope following the shock of a cancer diagnosis of a child. Parents who slept on mattresses or makeshift beds or on chairs as they tried to nod off for a few hours. Parents who travelled long distances and had nowhere to sleep, who were financially limited in what they could pay for accommodation for weeks on end. In the most difficult of times when families needed to be together they were split and children were left at home without their parents. So much pressure on top of a struggle to beat serious illness.

Along with his experience as a businessman, Bob Woodward now used his sad new role as the parent of a seriously ill child to make things better. Walking the walk enabled him to fight with determination to make this charity succeed.

The first practical was taken in 1974 with the purchase of a two-bedroomed bungalow in Frenchay Bristol. This was a place where parents could simply rest and recharge their batteries before returning to their daily routine in the hospital. It soon became apparent that accommodation was needed closer to the hospital and so a three-storey family home in Fremantle Square was purchased.

It was here that CLIC opened its heart to us as a family, and a big family at that, all arriving at all times from Cork. I first went one afternoon with Bernadette and Austin and Sarah, the CLIC nurse, for a quick look, as so many of the parents on the ward urged me to see how much support it proffered. The house was just a five-minute walk from the hospital, and as we entered I could sense that the atmosphere was not one of doom and gloom but bright and cheery. Jo Harding, the house manager, warmly welcomed us, a gentle kind woman who dedicated her time with such passion to families like us. The house was spic and span, with everything wonderfully organised throughout. The kitchen was warm and homely, and each family was assigned different sections of the fridge and encouraged to cook meals rather than grabbing ready-made foods and sandwiches, of which we were all truly sick of. There was a lounge and TV room, and most importantly a beautiful, fully equipped toy room for children allowed out of hospital for a short while to play with their siblings and have a break, a chance to experience a few hours of family normality. The family bedrooms were like those of a first-class hotel, and it was soon a welcomed place to grab a few hours' sleep, or simply sit alone in quite in an effort to renew strength. How I soon worshipped our time with Aaron in the house.

CLIC House made life so much easier as regards the practical day-to-day needs, but more than that it was a place where the experiences of each and every family were respected and accepted, regardless of their point in the journey. There were times when I desperately needed to be with other families sitting in the kitchen discussing the daily happenings on the oncology ward. We held each other together, a bond that brought strangers into each other's worlds, clutching each other's pain.

The kitchen, the heart of most homes, was a place of chatter and laughter, a place where you were never isolated, a place where everyone knew that by being there they were not alone, they had someone to talk to. But there were times when all you needed was to be left alone. Many a time I would just pass by the kitchen, unable to go in. This was never seen as a snub but accepted as an indication that the day was not going well – there were no words needed.

CLIC allowed me to be where I needed to be and I know today that my experience within this amazing world of care has made me a better person.

It was also very important to be surrounded by family and to see familiar faces. Even though we had good friends in Taunton, at times of crisis it is natural to want to be in the bosom of one's family. It is only when life deals one a traumatic blow that one fully appreciates the bond within a family. I was extremely lucky for the love and concern shown to us by my own brothers and sisters and my parents, whom I know struggled tremendously with their own sadness.

CLIC House allowed us to be together and I started to notice very early a roster of visits from Ireland developing: as soon as one brother or sister left, within a short period another would arrive, and this ensured that each had their own individual time with us, never all at once but practically organised so that we were never alone nor overwhelmed.

During their time at CLIC House family members were so in awe of the wonderful welcome they received and the friendly atmosphere within the house. Charlie, my brother, was truly amazed by this wonderful facility and how it relieved parents of so much pressure, both financially and practically. In the years following Aaron's death we often recalled our time in Bristol, remembering staff and other parents and children. It didn't surprise me when, thirteen years later, Charlie contacted me saying that he had been approached by the Knights of Columbanus who wanted to give financial backing to a community project. Charlie, a Garda Inspector, had been involved in establishing many community projects, but following his time in CLIC he had always been inspired to bring a similar facility to Cork, and now the timing was right. Having built up a successful reputation as a community project leader he soon became fully immersed in bringing this dream to life.

He approached the city council, who donated land at Cardinal Court, Wilton, a perfect location to begin this project, within a five-minute walk of Cork University Hospital. Families who travelled for miles to be with ill family members had been sleeping at bedsides in the hospital or in bed and breakfasts, a financial burden when the care involved long-term stays. Children had to travel for treatments and parents were exhausted with the daily demands placed upon them. Remembering how great a difference CLIC House made to the valuable time we had with Aaron, Charlie felt it was important for any family wanting to be with loved ones at difficult times, to be relieved of some of the worries that might impede on their precious time. By 2005 the house known as Brú Columbanus was compleated. Now the families of seriously ill children in Cork had somewhere warm and welcoming where they could relax and feel at home. I felt so proud that Charlie honoured his time with Aaron, and through his good work in the years following his nephew's death he remained connected to him.

The board of management consists of professionals who through their individual expertise work tirelessly for An Brú Columbanus. The Department of Health, under Micheál Martin at the time, contributed a substantial amount, realising the positive impact such a facility would have on families availing of this home away from home. Successful fund-raising saw major contributions from businesses both big and small, each valuable to the dream.

Brú consists of twenty-four family rooms containing bedrooms and small lounges. There are kitchens on each of the floors, as well as laundry rooms, counselling rooms, TV rooms, board rooms, prayer rooms, play rooms and offices. Staff include managers, receptionists and local volunteers who all contribute to the running of this house.

It was in the prayer room of Brú Columbanus on 27 September that I unveiled a plaque in remembrance of Aaron. Today Brú Columbanus is indeed a story of good emerging from pain and loss, and it encompasses a remembrance of and gratitude for all those who remain in our hearts. Now, thirteen years after Aaron's death, I can smile, and, most importantly, thank the God I battled with for bestowing on us the privilege of being the chosen parents and family to this wonderful young boy who has through his short life enriched our lives and has left a legacy of compassion and goodness, a gift from Bristol to Cork, from Aaron to home.

I am often asked if I still miss Aaron and if I wonder what he would be like today. Of course I sometimes try to visualise the teenager he would be and the brotherly relationship he would have with Colin. But miss him? Never. How can I miss my darling son who has never left me for one moment, his presence embracing those entering the doors of Brú House. It is through the wonderful support, warmth and compassion extended to the families in their time of need that Aaron continues to live.

CHAPTER X

—◦◦◦—

The prayer room in Brú is a haven of tranquillity and solace for those who today are experiencing difficult times due to the ill health of a loved one. It is a wonderful place of comfort, or for time alone to be with one's thoughts. The peaceful atmosphere enables one to gather strength to continue the journey, or simply to shed tears. It is a joyous place of thanks for those successful stories of recovery, and a stop-off point for people to contemplate the true values in life.

My hope is that those parents who come to spend time here, upon glancing at the beautiful plaque remembering Aaron, will be inspired by his dignity and will recognise the amazing work of Brú Columbanus that keeps his spirit alive.

The years following Aaron's loss have passed by so quickly. He certainly made way for his beautiful sisters, Chloe and Ava, each of whom share his wonderful sense of fun. Colin is now twenty years old and I know how much he still misses his brother. He often comments about how Aaron must be laughing at his suffering amongst women.

Time doesn't ease the pain. You constantly try to make sense of something that will never make sense. We now often wonder what Aaron would be like if he were still with us today. A teenager, fourteen years old, now in secondary school, and I know those beautiful blue eyes and golden hair would have many a girl's heart broken. Maybe he would play rugby or soccer; maybe he would be a fan of Man United. What music would he like? What experiences and arguments would he have with his brother? Though I try to bring him with us in time, I still have such a strong sense of him as my baby boy. I often smile when asked how much I miss him, as time has replaced our sense of loss with a stronger sense of his presence. Though I cannot touch him I know I am never without him.

I recall some time after his death asking him just to let me know that he was happy and still with us. Some nights later I dreamt I saw him sitting at the end of a long corridor in his bouncer kicking his legs, looking excited and laughing brightly. When I woke I turned to Austin and told him that Aaron was just fine. It was the first peaceful feeling I had in a long time. Today I do not fear my own death for I know what a privilege it will be to have Aaron placed once more in my arms.

My anger with God has been replaced by an acceptance, and I know now that the good I was once told would come from our pain has blossomed. Ours is a place of acceptance, the sense of which I hope I can pass on to those parents who now stuggle with the serious illness of a child.

I don't know why you have been chosen to travel your own journey. I don't know how to ease your pain. I don't have answers to all your doubts and fears. I don't know how to justify to you the unfairness of it all. But I do know that within you there is such an abundance of love given to you by God, and from this comes remarkable strength, a strength each of us shares, and this is our true legacy.